GREED
& Its Rewards

SIN SERIES

VOLUME III

Greed

& Its Rewards

DREW FETHERSTON

RED ROCK PRESS, NEW YORK

Copyright © 2000, by Red Rock Press
ISBN: 0-9669573-3-4
Library of Congress: 00-190831
Published by Red Rock Press
New York, New York
U.S.A.
www.redrockpress.com

Grateful acknowledgement is made for use of the following art:

Cover: *Alto Riesgo (High Risk)* by Ernesto Bertani, 70 cm. X 120 cm., 1993. Courtesy of Zurbaran, El Arte de los Argentinos, Buenos Aires.

Back cover: *Allegory of Fortune* by Dosso Dossi, circa 1530. Courtesy of J. Paul Getty Museum, Los Angeles.

Every reasonable effort has been made to trace and credit the ownership of any copyright-protected material appearing in this book. Any errors are inadvertent and will be corrected in subsequent editions if the publisher is notified of the mistake.

PRINTED IN HONG KONG

TABLE OF CONTENTS

CHAPTER ONE

RICH &

RICHER

In days of yore there were only a few good roads to wealth. The best one was the royal one: If you could arrange to be the firstborn to a king and queen, your path to a monarch's emoluments was straight and sure—unless or until the next coup separated you from your money, and your head from your body.

The other high road to high living was the military one, although in the bad old days, king and warrior were often one and the same—recall how Agamemnon gloried in the title, "Sacker of Cities." The plunder road often led straight to a throne, although it might take a swipe of the battle-axe to persuade a reigning monarch to step aside.

In those violent times, strict accounting was difficult. It's hard to calculate the size of ancient fortunes in modern terms, or to decide whether Despot A had more in his treasure room than Sacker-of-Cities B.

Civilization opened some new roads to wealth—not as bloody as the old ones, although money still tended to accumulate in a few fortunate hands. Today, however, it's easier to figure out who's got more than whom.

Sword Play

One master plunderer was Moorish warrior Al-Mansour (938-1002), who made a habit of sacking Spain; he amassed enough gold to build a palace, known as the "Shining City."

Machmud of Ghazni, his Afghani counterpart, invaded India annually for a quarter-century, returning each time with magnificent jewels and slaves. One excursion yielded so many slaves that prices plunged in the human-flesh markets. Machmud had a fine collection of erotic manuscripts and a palace with room enough for 400 poets. He gave one bard three mouthfuls of pearls for a verse he particularly liked.

Born Businessmen

Some of the bygone rich made their money the new-fashioned way: They earned it in commerce. However, getting started required a good stake, and a throne and crown were the equivalents of today's MBA from Harvard or Wharton.

Tenkaminin, A 10th-Century caliph of Ghana, exported enough gold, ivory and salt to put precious glass windows in his palace, to dress only in silk, and to tether his horses with gold rings. Since he liked the look of gold, he kept the largest nuggets to decorate his home.

Although the Byzantine Emperor Basil II was known as *Bulgaroctonus* ("Bulgar Slayer") for his 1014 military victory over the Bulgar Czar Samuel, he'd acquired much of his considerable fortune—his treasury held 300,000 pounds of gold—in peaceful trade, particularly of silk. He lived simply and ruled well.

Theft in the Name of God

The wealth Basil II bequeathed to his successors drew the covetous gaze of the Crusaders, who sacked Constantinople in 1204. It was an orgy of greed. "How can I begin to tell of the deeds wrought by these nefarious men!" lamented the Byzantine chronicler, Nicetas Choniates. "They snatched the precious reliquaries, thrust into their bosoms the ornaments these contained, and used the broken remnants for pans and drinking cups."

After stripping the great church of St. Sophia of its gold and silver, the crusaders stabled horses and mules under its magnificent dome.

"In the alleys, in the streets, in the temples, complaints, weeping, lamentation, grief, the groaning of men, the shrieks of women, wounds, rape and captivity," Nicetas wrote. "Oh, immortal God, how great the afflictions of the men, how great the distress!"

Angor Wat

Castles with Caché

The dark of the 12th Century still cloaked Europe when Suryavarman II of Cambodia built Angkor Wat, largely with the wealth he earned exporting kingfisher feathers to China. The trade was lucrative enough for him to build a palace with a tower of copper and another of gold, which one approached over a gold bridge guarded by gold lions. He rode in a gold howdah on his elephant, who had gold-sheathed tusks.

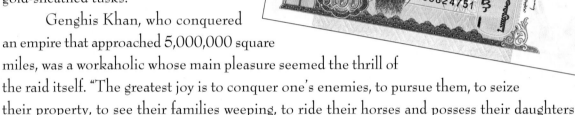

Genghis Khan, who conquered an empire that approached 5,000,000 square miles, was a workaholic whose main pleasure seemed the thrill of the raid itself. "The greatest joy is to conquer one's enemies, to pursue them, to seize their property, to see their families weeping, to ride their horses and possess their daughters and wives," he advised.

His grandson, Kubla Khan, used his considerable inheritance to build a jeweled palace that astounded Marco Polo and became an inspiration for Coleridge.

In Xanadu did Kubla Khan
A stately pleasure dome decree:
Where Alph, the sacred river, ran
Through caverns measureless to man
Down to a sunless sea . . .
—Samuel Taylor Coleridge, *Kubla Khan*

"When a man tells you he got rich through hard work, ask him whose."
—DON MARQUIS

FATAL CONNECTIONS

The Renaissance opened doors for entrepreneurs with connections in high places, although such patronage could prove toxic. Jacques Coeur, a French merchant of the 15th Century, made enough money to lend King Charles VII nearly a ton of gold to drive out the English. His reward was to be falsely accused of murder; Charles confiscated his properties.

The Japanese trader Yodoya Tatsugoro amassed a fortune that included 73 tons of gold, 292 tons of silver, 250 farms and warehouses full of luxury goods. The government (whose members owed him money) confiscated his fortune as "unbecoming" in 1705.

"The way to wealth is as plain as the way to the market. It depends chiefly on two words, industry and frugality; that is waste neither time nor money but make the best of both."
—BENJAMIN FRANKLIN

The Way We Were

"I never met in America with any citizen so poor as not to cast a glance of hope and envy on the enjoyments of the rich, or whose imagination did not possess anticipation of those good things that fate still obstinately withheld from him . . .

"I never perceived among the wealthier inhabitants of the United States that proud contempt of physical gratifications which is sometimes to be met with even in the most opulent and dissolute aristocracies. Most of these wealthy persons were once poor; they have felt the sting of want; they were long a prey to adverse fortunes; and now that the victory is won, the passions which accompanied the contest have survived it: their minds are, as it were, intoxicated by the small enjoyments which they have pursued for forty years . . . The love of well-being is now become the predominant taste of the nation; the great current of men's passions runs in that channel, and sweeps everything along in its course." —ALEXIS DE TOCQUEVILLE, *Democracy in America*, 1839

"The people of this country are not jealous of fortunes, however great, which have been built up by the honest development of great enterprises, which have been actually earned by business energy and sagacity; they are jealous only of speculative wealth, of the wealth which has been piled up by no effort at all, but only by shrewd wits playing on the credulity of others . . . This is predatory wealth and is found in the stock markets." —WOODROW WILSON, 1909

John D. Rockefeller—ready for an auto ride.

You Think I'm Rockefeller?

Who are the richest Americans? How did the Rockefeller fortune compare with that of Bill Gates?

Writers Michael Klepper and Robert Gunther made a careful effort to weigh some of the great U.S. fortunes against others—by estimating the size of each fortune, adding back any amounts given to charity, comparing it to the estimated Gross National Product of the time, correcting the sums for inflation. Here's their rich-guy ranking:

1. **John D. Rockefeller**, born in 1839, built a $900 million fortune by 1913; this represented $1/44$th of the GNP—the equivalent of $190 billion today. By 1922, the oil baron had given away about $1 billion to charity and relatives, keeping about $20 million. He died in 1937. Rockefeller's company, Standard Oil, was the grandfather of Exxon.

2. **Andrew Carnegie**, born in 1835, rose from railroad telegrapher to steel executive, and by 1901 was worth $250 million, $1/83$rd of the GNP. In current currency, that would be a shade more than $100 billion. He gave almost all of it away before his death in 1919. His money built more than 2,000 libraries.

3. **Cornelius Vanderbilt**, born in 1794, began by running a Staten Island ferry serv-

BRAUN POST CARD CO., CLEVELAND

ice and became a steamship and railroad tycoon, amassing a $105 million fortune—$1/187$th of the GNP, worth about $96 billion in today's dollars. He kept the money in the family, leaving most of it to his son, William, at his death in 1877.

4. **William H. Gates III**, born 1955, had made $90 billion, by the late 1990's, in shaping the computer industry, via Microsoft, according to his exceptional vision. He has already given large chunks of it away.

5. **Stephen Girard**, born 1750, began as a cabin boy and built a fleet of merchant vessels, then moved on to land, insurance and banking to build a $7.5 million fortune—equivalent to $1/150$th of the young nation's GNP. Adjusted for inflation, his fortune was more than $55.6 billion. He died in 1831.

6. **Alexander T. Stewart**, a Scotch-Irish immigrant born in 1803, revolutionized retailing in his New York department stores and thereby built a $5,000 inheritance into $50 million, $1/178$th of the GNP. Value today: about $47 billion. He died in 1876.

7. **Frederick Weyerhaeuser**, born in Germany in 1834, started as a sawmill helper in Illinois, became a foreman and, in time, a lumber baron worth $200 million—about $43.2 billion in today's dollars, equivalent to $1/193$rd of the GNP. He died in 1914.

RICHES ARE . . .

"A gift from heaven signifying, 'This is my beloved son in whom I am well pleased.'
—JOHN D. ROCKEFELLER.

"The reward of toil and virtue.'
—J. P. MORGAN

—AMBROSE BIERCE, *THE DEVIL'S DICTIONARY*

8. **Jay Gould**, born poor in 1836, began buying stock in small railroad lines in the early 1860s and in 20 years controlled 15,000 miles of track. In 1869, he conspired with others to gain control of the gold market, provoking the "Black Friday" panic that ruined thousands of smaller fry but from which he profited enormously. He built a $72 million bundle (1/198th of the GNP) that today would be worth more than $42 billion. Some of this grand sum was frittered away, after Jay's death in 1892, by his daughter Anna, a tale told in the chapter, "Hey, Big Spender."

9. **Marshall Field**, born 1834, began as an errand boy and became a Chicago department store magnate worth $140 million–$40.7 billion in current funds, then equal to 1/205th of GNP. He coined the phrase, "The customer is always right." He died in 1892.

10. **Sam Walton** built a small retail business into Wal-Mart and a personal fortune of $28 billion (1/223rd of GNP) before his death in 1992. Inflation makes it worth $37.4 billion today.

Few of the Founding Fathers had monumental wealth, even in the days when the GNP came mostly from farms. **George Washington** did make the list, at No. 59, and **Ben Franklin** who took some of the thrift-and-industry advice he dished out in *Poor Richard's Almanac*, ranked 86th.

J. P. Morgan, by the way, ranked 23rd. But it's surprising how little remembered are many of the list. Who recalls **Elias Hasket Derby** (No. 39) or **James C. Flood** (No. 32) or **John L. Blair** (No. 20)? The only woman on the top 100 is **Hetty Green**, known as "The Witch of Wall Street," whose eccentricities are chronicled in another chapter.

WORLD OF WEALTH

As the 21st Century unrolls, who in the world holds the most marbles? According to Forbes the winner is **Bill Gates**—whose fortune in the year, 2000, had dwindled to a mere $60 billion, thanks to the justice department's threat to break up Microsoft. Weighing in after Gates, is Oracle founder **Larry Ellison**, at $47 billion. Tied, with $28 billion each in the personal kitty: American investor **Warren Buffet** and Microsoft cofounder **Paul Allen**.

German retailers **Theo & Karl Albrecht**, Saudi Prince **Alwaleed Bin Talal Alsaud** and U.S. discount shopping king **S. Robert Walton** could each count $20 billion in his coffer. Japanese software magnate **Masayoshi Son** came on $19.4 billion strong, while **Michael Dell's** computer profits brought his worth to $17.8 billion. In the number 10 slot: Canadian media magnate **Kenneth Thomson**–$16.1 billion.

Die Goldwägerin (Woman Weighing Gold) by Jan van Hemmesen (1500-1556)

THE QUEEN TAKES HER SHOT

The richest person in Britain in 2000 was worth a mere $6.4 billion, and he wasn't even English, *The Sunday Times* reported, pegging the worth of Swedish industrialist and packaging tycoon **Hans Rausing** at £4 billion. The Swede was followed by a true English blueblood, the **Duke of Westminster**, worth the equivalent of $6 billion, thanks to owning huge chunks of the London neighborhoods of Mayfair and Belgravia.

Meanwhile, the Queen of England is trying to catch up with dot.com millionaires. **Elizabeth II** is said to be a private investor, to the tune of £100,000, in a company called getmapping.com.

> "At the end of the game, the king and the pawn go in the same box."
> —Italian proverb

Top Wage Slaves

A merica's 10 highest-paid (total compensation, including salary, bonuses, and long-term compensation) chief executives, as calculated by *Business Week* in 1999:

Michael Eisner, Walt Disney	$575,592,000
Mel Karmazin, CBS	$ 201,934,000
Sanford Weill, Citigroup	$ 167,093,000
Stephen Case, America Online	$ 159,233,000
Craig Barrett, Intel	$ 116,511,000
John Welch, General Electric	$ 83,664,000
Henry Schacht, Lucent Technologies	$ 67,036,000
L. Dennis Kozlowski, Tyco International	$ 65,264,000
Henry Silverman, Cendant	$ 63,882,000
M. Douglas Ivester, Coca-Cola	$ 57,322,000

One woman made the top 20: **Margaret Whitman** of Ebay, who pulled in $43 million.

Most of the compensation—on average, two-thirds—comes from stock options, which dilute the worth of a company's stock, sometimes with harsh results. A study of 100 big companies turned up 11 in which profit turned to loss when the options were considered. One stark example occurred in 1998, when Computer Associates' CEO Charles Wang received shares worth $670 million, thereby turning a quarterly profit of $194.2 million into a loss of $480.8

million for the company. When the news reached investors, the company stock lost nearly a third of its value in a single day.

Are the execs worth this kind of cash? A 1999 survey of the 365 largest U.S. companies found that their profits dropped 1.4 percent—while CEO pay rose 36 percent.

WELCOME TO THE GAP

In 1980, according to *Business Week's* reckoning, the Chief Executive Officer of a major corporation made about 42 times as much as a typical American factory worker. By 1990, the gap had widened to 85 times. By 1998, it had increased to a staggering 419 times as much.

Want to know what you'd be making now and over the next couple of years if your salary increased as rapidly as the average CEO's? The AFL-CIO, using *Business Week's* figures, came up with a calculator. Find your 1994 salary in the top rank, then read down to see what your paycheck would look like.

1994	$ 20,000	$ 40,000	$ 60,000	$ 80,000	$ 100,000
1997	$ 54,148	$ 108,296	$ 162,445	$ 216,593	$ 270,741
2000	$ 145,885	$ 291,770	$ 437,656	$ 583,541	$ 729,427
2001	$ 203,710	$ 407,420	$ 611,131	$ 814,841	$ 1,018,552
2002	$ 284,455	$ 568,911	$ 853,367	$ 1,137,823	$ 1,422.278
2003	$ 397,206	$ 794,412	$ 1,191,618	$ 1,588,825	$ 1,986,031

If things continue this way, the AFL-CIO analysts note, CEOs will make 150,000 times more than the average factory worker by the year 2050.

No Trespassing!

Land ownership, like cash, isn't evenly distributed among the citizenry. *Worth* magazine figured out that the cumulative holdings of just 100 individuals equal more than one percent of the United States. Here are the top land barons:

1. **Ted Turner**, the Georgia media mogul, owns 1.3 million acres in various states, including 1.15 million in New Mexico, about one and a half percent of the state.

2. **Red Emmerson**, California timber baron, owns about 1.3 million acres.

3. **Henry Singleton**, co-founder of Teledyne, is said to own about 1.1 million acres in New Mexico, plus a 45,000-acre ranch in

VASE, CIRCA 1500 B.C., FROM THE LITTLE PALACE AT KNOSSOS.

California's Salinas Valley.

    4. Seventy members of the Pingree family, whose ancestors started buying New England land in 1820, retain about 975,000 acres of Maine woods.

    5. King Ranch heirs own 860,000 acres in Texas, Florida and Kentucky. Steamboat captain Richard King began buying land (for as little as two cents an acre) in 1853.

> "Superfluous wealth can buy superfluities only."
> —HENRY DAVID THOREAU,
> *On Walden Pond*

CHAPTER TWO
THE SOUL

WARS

oesn't the Bible say that money is the root of all evil? Not exactly. St. Paul actually says, "For the love of money is the root of all evil; it is through this craving that some have wandered away from the faith." –*NT, I Timothy* 6:10

And Paul concludes in the same letter to Timothy, "As for the rich in this world, charge them not to be haughty, nor to set their hopes on uncertain riches but on God who richly furnishes us with everything to enjoy. They are to do good, to be rich in good deeds, liberal and generous." –6:17-18

Most major religions contain the seeds both for the celebration of wealth and the condemnation of *unbridled* craving for riches.

The precepts of most faiths recognize that human beings have a deep, legitimate wish for contentment, and that abundance is a powerful aid to happiness. If all springs from God, then taking pleasure in His bounty may be seen as gratitude. Moreover, several faiths praise the sober ethic and labor that one needs to make money.

Avarice, 1904, by James Ensor.

When amassing wealth becomes an end in itself, it's sinful because it's an obsession that impedes higher striving; hoarding replaces charity; lust for others' possessions sparks lying, stealing and even murder.

The shine of gold is so blinding, though, that even wise men blur distinctions between just wealth and filthy lucre. Rare is the text that's not contradictory about earthly riches. And while the ideals of all faiths soar above material desire, Buddhism, while lauding generosity, seems the most consistent in its disdain for worldly treasure.

Rewards Here and Now

"If thou shalt hearken unto the voice of the Lord . . . the Lord shall make thee plenteous in goods, in the fruit of thy body, and in the fruit of thy cattle, and in the fruit of thy ground . . . The Lord shall open unto thee his good treasure." *OT, Deuteronomy 28*

"Every man also to whom God hath given riches and wealth . . . this is the gift of God." *–OT, Ecclesiastes 5:19*

"If the search for riches is sure to be successful, though I should become a groom with whip in hand to get them, I will do so. As the search may not be successful, I will follow after that which I love." –CONFUCIUS, *Analects*

Proverbial Wisdom

"Food gained by fraud tastes sweet to a man, but he
ends up with a mouth full of gravel."
–OT Proverbs 20:17

"A generous man will prosper; he who refreshes others
will himself be refreshed." –11:25

"Lazy hands make a man poor, but diligent hands bring wealth." –10:4

"Riches certainly make themselves wings; they fly away as an eagle toward heaven."–23:5

"He that hateth covetousness shall prolong his days." –27:16

"He that maketh haste to be rich shall not be innocent."
–28:20

"Renounce and enjoy."
–Mohandas Gandhi

Words From on High

"And [Jesus] said to his disciples: 'Do not seek what you are to eat or what you are to drink or be of anxious mind. For all nations of the world seek these things, and your Father knows you need them. Instead, seek His kingdom, and these things shall be yours as well.'"
—*NT, Luke 12:29-30*

"Our Lord commonly giveth riches to such gross asses to whom he affordeth nothing else that is good."
—MARTIN LUTHER, *Colloquies*

It Would Take a Miracle

"It is easier for a camel to go through the eye of a needle than for a rich man to enter the kingdom of God."Jesus, —*NT Matthew* 19:23; *Mark* 10:25; *Luke* 18:25

After Jesus pronounced this, his amazed disciples asked, "Who can then be saved?" The gospels agree on the sense of Jesus' reply: What is impossible for men is possible for God.

Mohammed on Money

The *Koran* treats wealth much as Judeo-Christian scripture does: as a sign of Allah's approval, as a snare and as an opportunity to please Allah through charity. Riches may also be a chimera.

"Let not their wealth nor their children dazzle thee: In reality Allah's wish is to punish them with these things in life, that their souls may perish in their denial of Allah." –*Koran 9:55*

"The parable of those who spend their wealth in the way of Allah is that of a grain of corn: It groweth seven ears, and each ear hath a hundred grains. Allah giveth manifold increase to whom He pleaseth." –*2:261*

"Wealth and sons are allurements of the life of this world: But the things that endure, good deeds, are best in the sight of thy Lord." –*18:46*

DETAIL OF PORCELAIN FIGURES, MUSEO DI SAN MARTINO, NAPLES

"So he who gives in charity and fears Allah
And in all sincerity testifies to the best
We will indeed make smooth for him the path to Ease.
But he who is a greedy miser and thinks himself self-sufficient,
And gives the lie to the best,
We will indeed make smooth for him the path to Misery
Nor will his wealth profit him when he falls into the Pit." —92:5

"Allah will admit those who believe and work righteous deeds, to Gardens beneath which rivers flow: they shall be adorned with bracelets of gold and pearls, and their garments there will be of silk." —22:23

Buddha Was Not a Material Guy

Buddhism is devoted to the achievement of nirvana, a pure, spiritual state, devoid of all desire. This is approached by the "eightfold path," which emphasizes compassion and self-denial. The *Dhammapada* consists of 423 verses, spoken by Buddha.

"Truly, misers fare not to heavenly realms; nor, indeed, do fools praise generosity. But the wise man rejoices in giving, and by that alone he becomes happy hereafter."

"Whoever is free from attachment knows neither grief nor fear. From greed comes grief; from greed comes fear."

"Cut down the forest of desires, not just a tree; danger is in the forest."

"One who looks upon the world as a bubble and a mirage, the King of Death sees not."

> "There is nothing holy about being poor."
> —BHAGWAN SHREE RAJNEESH, (whose followers bought him 27 Rolls Royces).

Hindu Holiness

The *Bhagavad Gita* takes the high road in its view of greed. Earthbound passion spawns uncontrollable hankering for, and attachment to, possessions—a guaranteed route to spiritual distress.

Condemned as greedy and impure is the worker who is attached to the fruits of his labor and who passionately wants to enjoy them. The person who has the possibility of ascending in a future life is "one who regards alike pleasure and pain, and looks on a clod, a stone and a piece of gold with an equal eye."

These spiritually refined formulations coexist in text and in popular observance with the older Vedic gods, including Lakshmi, the goddess of wealth and fortune, power and beauty.

Devotion to Lakshmi (sometimes called Sri) runs deep and strong in India and other Hindu communities. And this temple goddess embodies—literally—a complex view of wealth and human existence.

Lakshmi has four hands, representing her power to grant the four types of *purusharthas*, or ends of human life: *dharma* (righteousness), *kama* (bodily pleasure), *moksha* (beatitude) and *artha* (wealth).

Wearing gold, and sitting on a lucky lotus blossom, she can assure agricultural abundance, bless businesses and dispense riches. Lakshmi doesn't require large deposits of rupees before showering wealth. Small offerings of cash on her altar may do the trick, especially during the *Lakshmi Divali*, the October festival of lights in her honor.

"In the very attempt to wrongly gain another's wealth, a man loses his family's future and his own faultlessness. Just as wise men know the goodness of non-coveting, so Fortune herself knows their goodness and draws near." —TIRUVALLUVAR, *Kural*

CHAPTER THREE

Hey, Big

Spender

"I get so tired of listening to one million dollars here, one million there," said a testy Imelda Marcos as critics tut-tutted about her extravagance. "It's all so petty."

Ms. Marcos reminds us that there are two sorts of rich folk: the ones who never have enough and don't know how to enjoy it, the misers; and the big spenders. The former first lady of the Philippines belongs firmly to the latter group. Had the credit card not existed, her shopping sprees would have stimulated its invention. Six strong men couldn't lug enough cash to finance one of her mornings in, say, Henri Bendel.

In a sense, she agreed with Elvis Presley who, in a philosophic moment observed, "Sharing money is what gives it its value." Or as another thinker put it, "Too many people miss the silver lining because they're expecting gold."

Herewith a tip of the silk top hat to some who understood that money is worthless unless spent.

You Are Where You Live

Houses have always been badges of status. Almost anyone, even the rankest impostor, could scrape up enough to dress like a king but only someone with the goods could build a palace.

Xi Wang-mu, the Chinese goddess of immortality and the personification of the feminine element *yin*, dwelt in a nine-story palace of jade in the Kun-lun mountains, near the Lake of Jewels,

Previous Page: *Les Grandes Eaux illumines au basin á Versailles*, 1864, by Eugène Lami

The Breakers, the Newport summer
cottage built for Cornelius Vanderbilt II

Above: Versailles Hall
Left: The Breakers Great Hall

surrounded by a wall of pure gold over a thousand miles long. *Xi Wang-mu* lived with the immortals, who drew their eternal life from the peach of immortality, which grew in her garden.

Many of the rich ever since have sought some sort of immortality in architecture. Louis XIV had pragmatic reasons for building *Versailles*—all those courtiers, all that state business—but it's hard to imagine what necessity dictated the Gilded Age extravagances that once lined New York's Fifth Avenue and Newport's waterfront.

One small detail can give an idea of the luxuries that were their hallmark: When financier Thomas F. Ryan built his 50-plus-room Fifth Avenue mansion about a century ago, his wife understandably wanted a rose garden. Ryan bought the adjoining and very opulent Yerkes mansion and tore it down to make room for a garden. He left a $50,000 marble staircase standing, though, as a trellis. Ryan was proud of his thrift. "That sort of thing can run into money if you build it from scratch," he said of his rose arbor.

Good as Gold

Instead of printing money, Boniface, Count de Castellane, made his by marrying it. His wife, Anna Gould, was one of Jay's six children, and thanks to Boni, the one who spent the most in the least amount of time.

Jay Gould had been such a master manipulator of Erie Railroad stock that the Erie had been known as "The Scarlet Woman of Wall Street." Gould, who once declared, "Any man can make a fortune but it takes a genius to hold onto it," raked it in so fast that living magnificently didn't dent his fortune. He died in 1892, leaving an estate that comprised $82,000,000 in liquid assets, land worth $12,000,000 and controlling interests in corporations worth $350,000,000.

Anna met Boni in Paris two years after her father's death. He was a busted French aristocrat and his genius was not of the sort that Gould would have admired. Boni had *brilliant* taste. Anna was charmed by him but not quite smitten enough to stand still. The count borrowed money (against future earnings) from a chum, followed the heiress to Newport, and married her not long after in New York.

For Boni, the marriage license was forged in gold, his passport to a life of delightful excess. He began with a custom-built yacht, the *Valhalla*—1,600 tons, requiring a crew of 90, plus eight officers.

Ashore, Boni pumped new life into the economy of the Faubourg St-Honoré, buying tapestries, wines, Sèvres, antiquities, Old Masters. He threw an outdoor party for 3,000 in the

Bois de Boulogne, on 15 kilometers of specially made carpet, with entertainment supplied by 200 musicians. The cost was something like $250,000.

> "Knowledge makes one laugh, but wealth makes one dance."
> —George Herbert, *Jacula Prudentum*

Superb as Boni's taste was—many of his purchases later found their way to great museums—his sense of household economy was deliriously deficient. Among the charms of his Parisian townhouse were a theater for 600 and a cold-storage system that allowed him to keep food on hand for 500 dinner guests.

Anna's brothers became alarmed, and in time Anna did too. When the outflow due to Boni's shopping sprees reached $12,000,000, they pulled the plug. (Asked what he spent the money on, Boni replied, "my general existence, my châteaux, my palaces, my *bibelots*, my race horses, my yachts, my traveling expenses, my political career, my charities, my fêtes, my wife's jewels and loans to my friends.")

Boni returned one evening to an empty house. He lived on in Paris for many years, fortunes diminished but taste intact, a famous figure on the boulevards. Anna married another, less costly French aristocrat.

Bigger Is Better

It's distressing but true: When it comes to building, many of the well-to-do (particularly those new to wealth) seem to feel that bigger is better. From the Hamptons to Hollywood, citizens have looked on in helpless dismay as lovely old homes were bought, bulldozed and replaced with 30,000 square-foot (and up) monstrous monuments to the new owners' bankbooks.

Sometimes it doesn't even require a teardown to get the juices of civic outrage flowing. In Southampton, New York, some residents are attempting to use zoning law to slam shut their ersatz barn doors before reclusive industrialist Ira Rennert turns blueprints into domestic bliss. Rennert's prospective residence has a floor plan of almost two acres, including 29 bedrooms and 40 bathrooms, two bowling alleys, a 165-seat movie theater, and parking for 200 cars. Tunnels will connect the residence to six outbuildings scattered around the 63-acre site. The cost? About $100 million. The tunnels, no doubt, will cut down on Rennert's umbrella bill.

Neighbors have told zoning officials that they're skeptical about the quiet businessman's claim that what he's constructing is simply a home for him, his wife and two grown daughters. Some have spread dark rumors that he plans to turn his beach shack into a religious retreat or a hotel. Rennert's lawyer countered. "It is a *big* single-family home, but it is a single-family home nevertheless."

Computer billionaire Bill Gates might agree. Gates built himself one of the grander houses of the 20th Century, a 66,000-square-foot compound (equivalent to an acre and a half) on a five-acre waterfront site on Seattle's Lake Washington. It comprises a mere seven bedrooms, but has 24 bathrooms, six kitchens and six fireplaces. It cost more than $50 million, and taxes run close to $650,000 a year.

Gates can afford it. There is a network of Internet pages dedicated to pondering the buying power of his fortune. Here are some conclusions:

• If Gates could manage to spend $120 a minute*, it would take ten centuries to spend it all. (That's if he kept it in his mattress and didn't earn any interest.)

* Not an impossible pace: Adnan Khashoggi, the Saudi oil-rich wheeler-dealer, was reputed to spend $300,000 a day—more than $200 a minute—when he was in full financial stride in the 1960s.

•Gates could send 577,000 deserving scholars to Harvard, where a degree costs about $137,000.

•Gates could buy 46.67 space shuttles.

•If Gates had 10-cents-a-minute phone service, he could talk for 1.5 million years.

•Or look at it this way: Say you're worth about $90,000 and take a date to the movies for $16. To make a similar dent in his wallet, Bill Gates would have to spend $14 million.

MONEY TO BURN

Ruminations on Gates' wealth illustrate a problem that bedevils the super-rich: It can be a real bitch to spend all that money. So many dollars, so little time. Perhaps that explains why a fair proportion of the rich end up as cranks and eccentrics. Consider, for example, James Gordon Bennett, the 19th-Century mogul who owned

CARTOON BY CLAUDE SERRE, EDITIONS GLÉNAT, GRENOBLE

The New York Herald and its Paris counterpart. Bennett was famous for the itch a wad of *francs* in his pocket produced.

Once, while interviewing a prospective employee in Paris, Bennett squirmed uncomfortably. Finally, he pulled a bankroll—all big bills—from his pocket and hurled it into the blazing fireplace. The interviewee leaped up, snatched the cash from the flames and handed it to Bennett, who again tossed the bills into the fire. "That's where I wanted them to be in the first place," he said.

He had no patience for the slightest discomfort. On New Year's Day, 1877, in his cups, Bennett urinated into the New York fireplace of his well-born fiancée. The young woman's brother responded by attempting to horsewhip Bennett in the street, prompting his target to challenge him to a duel, which duly took place in Maryland. No blood was shed, but it was the last recorded duel in U.S. history.

Bennett's Parisian sojourns were stamped with outbursts that doubled as unorthodox spending opportunities. He liked to enter a grand restaurant—*Maxim's* or *Voisin*, say—grab the tablecloths right and left, sending glasses and food-filled plates crashing onto the floor. Then he'd immediately and graciously pay for everything to soothe any injured feelings.

Even when bereft of scene-making occasions, Bennett was generous. He once tipped the sleeping-car porter on the *Train Bleu* to Monte Carlo 20,000 *francs*. He tossed a $100,000 check into the cradle of a distant nephew, and never saw the beneficiary again.

In 1900, Bennett built his yacht, the *Lysistrata*, for the then-astounding sum of $625,000. It had a Turkish bath on one of its three decks, and a padded stall for the ship's cow. Bennett liked fresh butter and milk punch for breakfast.

When the *Herald* moved uptown to Herald Square, Bennett commissioned a palace to receive it. Surviving are the $200,000 clock and two figures that strike the hours on a gong.

Bennett hoped to outmaneuver any discomfort of the hereafter by planning his eternal home—a million-dollar, Stanford White-designed mausoleum, in the shape of a 200-foot-tall owl, on his Washington Heights property, not far from Grant's Tomb. His plan collapsed when the philandering architect was murdered by a jealous husband. Bennett is buried outside Paris, under a mortal-sized headstone.

Royalty Has Its Privileges

When he declared himself Emperor of Central Africa in 1977, Jean-Bedel Bokassa duplicated the festivities that had attended Napoleon's coronation. The bill came to $25 million, equal to about 75 percent of his nation's annual exports.

Rebel with a Cause

"Colonel" Ned Green, the hulking, one-legged son of one of the all-time-great cheapskates, Hetty Green, took it to heart that living well is the best revenge. The colonel had reason to feel a wee bit bitter about his mom's economies. This immensely wealthy woman—she was worth more than $100 million when she died in 1916—hesitated to spend

money on a doctor when her son's leg was badly infected—hence his lost limb.

Ned owned a 35-foot boat with a 130-horse-power engine; it was one of the ten lifeboats on his 265-foot yacht, the *United States*, which had a crew of 73. He seems to have thought train travel a mite unsafe. Before leaving Florida to journey by railroad to Massachusetts, he stashed $1 million in cash and valuables in a shoebox and sent it ahead by American Express.

Otherwise, the colonel liked to keep a portion of his assets at hand. Once, while Ned was breakfasting in a Dallas hotel with a local banker, a messenger arrived with the news that there was a run on the Texan's bank. Ned whipped out his wallet and peeled off twenty $10,000 bills.

When it appeared this wasn't enough to paper the flow from his friend's bank, he sent a bellboy up to his room to bring down a battered valise. Ned opened the suitcase, counted out another thirty $10,000 notes, bringing the total to $500,000, then sent the still well-stocked case back upstairs with the bellboy.

IMPULSE PURCHASE

On his way through Paris to catch a train to Cherbourg, to board the *Mauretania* for a voyage to New York, international banker Jules Bache had his chauffeur stop to fetch some cigars from the humidors of a famous art gallery. While he waited, his fancy was taken by a Van

Dyck. Bache made the train with the cigars—and the $275,000 painting—under his arm.

No Business Like Show Business

W.C. Fields lived well but was obsessively fearful of being poor again.

If there's an excuse for mega-star miserliness it's this: *Many used to be poor.* W.C. Fields lived high-off-the-hog on his earnings, maintaining his heft with stylish victuals and serious booze, while dressing it up in custom-tailored English suits. He didn't mind spending dough on his favorite comedian, as long as he could make sure that, come what may, he had plenty left. During World War II, he had a secret bank account in Berlin, in case Philadelphia was on the losing side. He also used false names to stash an estimated $1 million in scores of bank accounts around the United States. He told friends that he maintained these accounts both as insurance against going broke, and as protection from the claims of kin whom he detested. But Fields didn't reveal his numerous *noms* de greenbacks. When he kicked the bucket in 1946, he left an $800,000 estate. The rest of his funds were never recovered.

JOHN DECKER FOR PARAMOUNT, 1936. FILM STILLS ARCHIVE, MUSEUM OF MODERN ART, NEW YORK

Another poverty-haunted star was Jackie Gleason, who feared he might again have to live in real life like a "honeymooner" or worse. At the height of his success he worried about its abrupt departure, and kept a trunk of clothing in New Jersey that he could grab should he have to get out of town fast.

Today's entertainers, who grew up outside the shadow of the Great Depression, are more comfortable with their great wealth. Witness Jerry Seinfeld, who retired when his sitcom was hot and tasty and was paying him $1 million per 30-minute episode. (To be fair, NBC made buckets of money on the show, and could well afford Jerry's paycheck.) Seinfeld, who had a normal suburban childhood, found the "retirement house" of his dreams in East Hampton and bought it—for something in excess of $35 million—from singer Billy Joel.

Flour Power

The Duke of Devonshire, running into debt in the early 1900s, brought in financial advisers to tell him how he might economize on his lavish lifestyle. One suggestion was that much could be saved in the kitchen: For instance, the advisers noted, he had three pastry chefs—French, Danish and Viennese—on his staff.

"Good God," cried the Duke. "Can't a man have a biscuit if he wants it?"

Looking Swell

In Depression-pinched 1935, smart-set scribe Lucius Beebe, who once described New York as "Babylon on the make," drew up an evening-clothes budget for a man-about-town:

Dress tailcoat suit	$ 325
Linen shirt, pique waistcoat, etc.	50
Dress dancing pumps	25
Silk or opera hat	30
Mink-lined greatcoat	2,500
Gloves	6
Muffler	20
Diamond and platinum pocket watch and chain	1,500
Cuff and shirt studs without jewels	350
Gold garters	150
Silk socks and underwear	20
TOTAL	$4,976

This was just for a single winter's night at the opera. No extra shirt or change of underwear was part of Beebe's calculation. And a gentleman's evening attire might well be embellished with such *objets* as a $1,500 gold cigarette case from Cartier or a *fouet*, a gem-studded whisk to stir the bubbles out of champagne.

KEEPING UP

In 1965, two years after the demise of Camelot on the Chesapeake, Eugenia Sheppard, fashion editor of *The New York Herald Tribune*, estimated that a woman in the social swirl needed to spend a minimum of $20,000 annually on her wardrobe, while a woman of greater means and ambition might easily spend $100,000, not counting jewelry and furs.

Here's what a woman had to have to look like a million dollars in mid-20th-Century New York:

Six suits, $1,000 to $2,000 each
Eight to ten matching coat-and-dress combinations, about $2,500 each
Six dinner dresses, about $1,000 each
Six ball gowns, $1,500 and up each
One deluxe fur coat from Revillon, about $75,000

A relatively hard-up fashion plate might have to make her fur last more than a single season, and cleverly have it refashioned into a lining for a cashmere cape when she acquired a coat with a fresher look. But the rest of her wardrobe would need to be replaced annually.

CHAPTER FOUR

FORTUNE'S

GODS

Our distant ancestors, being struggling farmers, naturally looked first to harvest deities for their luck. When the crops were safely in the barn, they looked to lesser gods for help in gambling and business. Luck became associated with talismans, charms and gestures, and while we may mock such naïve efforts to bring fortune, who among us has never carried a rabbit's foot, a lucky coin, a four-leaf clover? Who has no "lucky" number?

MAGIC COMES TO MIDAS

The Midas Touch was the gift of a god, a gift you might not want if you knew the whole story. Midas, in about 700 B.C., was at the top of the heap as king of Phrygia, which is in present-day Turkey. His treasure was his rose garden, where one day he found the satyr, *Silenus*, dead drunk.

The king nursed *Silenus* through a colossal hangover, and the grapevine god, *Dionysus*, decided to thank him by granting one special request. Faced with this Olympian offer, Midas forgot all about flowers and wished that anything he touched would turn to gold. *Dionysus* warned Midas that his desire might have unforeseeable consequences. But Midas held fast and his wish was granted.

The king worked up an appetite transforming all that surrounded him to gold, and then realized that he could not eat or drink. Worse, he accidentally touched his daughter and turned her to glittering, dead metal.

Midas pleaded with *Dionysus* to lift this curse, and the god told him to bathe in the headwaters of the Pactolus River. When he did, the river carried away the magic touch; the gold settled in the sands, which were carried downstream to Lydia.

Archaeologists recently completed tests on food and crockery fragments found in what may well have been Midas' tomb at Gordion, once Phrygia's capital. They concluded that the mourners drank *kykeon*, a Dionysian punch of wine, beer and mead.

RICH AS CROESUS

Croesus—who may have been the first ruler to mint coins—had the good luck to be King of Lydia, about a century after Midas' bath had flooded the territory with gold.

Croesus' wealth and his rich court at Sardis were the envy of the ancient world. And he was a fabled host.

One guest was the lawgiver, Solon. When Croesus asked Solon to identify the three happiest men he had known, Solon named three obscure dead men.

"Dost thou count my own happiness as nothing?" Croesus demanded.

"In truth, I count no man happy until his death," said Solon. "For no man can know what the gods have in store for him."

When Cyrus the Great of Persia threatened Lydia, Croesus consulted the Delphi oracle. The oracle's message was that if Croesus went to war, he would destroy a mighty empire. Heartened, he decided on attack.

Left: *Croesus Showing Solon His Treasures*, by Frans Francken the Younger (1586-1642)

Only after the battle was joined did Croesus realize that the oracle had been referring to Lydia. Cyrus was about to set his defeated foe on fire when Croesus remembered Solon's words, and cried out the revered lawgiver's name. Cyrus was moved enough to spare Croesus, as he grabbed the richest kingdom on earth.

FAST MOVER

Hermes was an ordinary fertility god until *Zeus* gave him winged sandals and made him his messenger. *Hermes'* speed appealed to mortals with special interests. He became the god of travel, communication, trade and wealth. *Hermes*, who was dubbed *Mercury* by the Romans, was also the patron saint of thieves.

> " **G**et place and wealth, if possible with grace. If not, by any means… Whatever prosperous hour Providence bestows upon you, receive it with a thankful hand, and defer not the enjoyment of the comforts of life."
>
> —HORACE, *Epistles*, Book I (c. 10 B.C.)

Right: *Mercury*, 1580, by Giovanni Da Bologna

Fortune Was a Female

In Rome, the goddess *Fortuna* was worshipped in a temple in the Forum Boarium and in a sanctuary on the Quirinal hill. She was portrayed richly dressed and often blindfolded to show fortune's impartiality. She or a handmaiden carried a cornucopia, a curved goat's horn overflowing with fruit and grain.

Ops (think opulence) was also adored. This goddess of abundance and wealth shared a temple in the Roman Forum with Ceres, as protectors of the harvest.

God of Deals

Veles, the Slavic deity of cattle traders, graduated to god of commercial prosperity as trade became more varied. Merchants, whatever they bought and sold, sealed their deals by oaths sworn in *Veles'* name.

THE JOSS GODS

Before Taoism and Buddhism arrived in China, there were deities for everything and everyone: gods to help farmers bring in a good harvest, gods who paid special attention to tailors, shoemakers, wine makers, clay sculptors. They were called upon to guard houses and businesses, and to confer good fortune. The door gods *Zhao Gongming* and *Ran Dengado* are the gods of wealth.

The tradition of burning joss for luck dates back to this polytheistic time. Traditionally, joss is made by carving the god's image on wood, then making paper prints from the wood blocks; the prints were burned as offerings.

In Taoism, the Heavenly Ruler was supposed to grant good fortune on his birthday, the fifteenth day of the first lunar month. On that day, the Chinese, particularly businessmen, offered sacrifices and prayed for good fortune. Some still do.

Chinese porcelains of *Three Stars*

Other wealth-oriented deities of Tao or Buddhist inspiration include the *Three Stars* (representing happiness, wealth and longevity) and the "God Bringing In Wealth and Treasures." There are seasonal good-luck prints entitled "Promotion to a Higher Rank," "Family Blessed with Good Fortune" and the "Horse of Emolument."

MAYAN MOOLAH MAN

Some Central Americans dote on images of a mustachioed man, in a black suit, red tie and broad-brimmed hat, seated in an armchair at a crossroads. This is *Maximon*, a.k.a. *Hermano San Simon*. *Maximon* is a meld of the Mayan wealth god, *Maam*, with St. Simon, dressed as one elegant *hombre*. He holds a baton in his right hand and gold coins in his left, and brings worldly success to devotees astute enough to offer him tobacco, alcohol and berries.

"O my son! I have eaten a bitter apple, and swallowed aloes, and I have found nothing more bitter than poverty and scarcity. O my son! A small fortune is better than a scattered fortune."
—AHIKAR, cupbearer to the Assyrian King Esarhaddon (c.700 B.C.).

Lady Bountiful

Mami Wata is a graceful East African water spirit who appears in dreams as a mermaid. But when she wanders among humans it is on her own two feet. She is one of the few wealth goddesses not linked to fertility. *Mami Wata's* sojourns on earth have made her ultra-sympathetic to human aspirations. Her fans offer her perfume and Coca Cola when they look to her for material comforts.

Mountain Magic

Ekkeko is a pre-Columbian abundance god who survives on his ability to improve the financial lot of adherents. Nowadays, the Andean deity is usually cast as a small plaster statue with a big smile on his face. Fully-loaded, a typical *Ekkeko* totes a bag of shredded green paper (representing good crops), a bag of rice, a clay cooking pot, small-denomination bills (or photocopies of U.S. dollars) and bags of sugar and herbs. On his back he may also carry a miniature house, panpipes and other symbols.

Wish charms must be affixed to *Ekkeko* before noon on January 24 to assure delivery by the end of the year.

HERE AND HEREAFTER

Wealth and death have cosmic links the world over. On Java, there is a demi-deity dragon known as the *naga*, who is the immensely wealthy king of the netherworld.

Hades, the Greek god of the underworld, was also called "The Rich One" because he ultimately owned the world.

In the Celtic pantheon, *Rosmerta* was goddess of abundance and queen of death. Gaulish images bestow upon her the Roman cornucopia of wealth, while her fatal attraction lies in her snake-twined stick.

As ideal mother and growth goddess, *Ala* symbolizes wealth for the Ibo of Nigeria and Gabon. She is also the guardian of the dead whom she welcomes back to her womb.

The connection between what you have and where you're headed may signify Death as Fortune Collector. Or maybe, as the pharaohs believed, you can take it with you. The mystery was summed up four and a half millennia ago:

There is no one who can return from there
To describe their nature, to describe their situation,
That he may quiet our desires
Until we reach the place that is the end.
—PHAHHOPTE, *Song of the Harper*

Ala, Growth goddess of Gabon

CLEARING THE PATH TO RICHES

The tool of the Yoruban god, *Ogun*, is a machete. *Ogun* is master of all metal; as such he is a war god and the guardian of both ironworkers and goldsmiths. When the deities first came to earth, the Nigerian story goes, they encountered an impenetrable thicket and were stymied until *Ogun* hacked it away. Thereafter, humans could prevail upon *Ogun* to slash away obstacles to prosperity. But if devotion to *Ogun* falls short, he may become irate and cause bloody accidents and quarrels.

Yoruban-rooted luck beliefs back the rites of Santeria, Macumba and Voodoo. Lighted green and yellow candles, representing paper currency and precious gold, are used to attract riches.

Some swear that the candles gain potency if shaped like a human skull, or

ILLUSTRATION BY CLAUDE SERRE, ÉDITIONS GLÉNAT, GRENOBLE

LE GRAND DIABLE MAMMON D'ARGENT
Patron de la Finance

MUSÉE CARNAVALET, PARIS, © GIANNE GAGLI ORTI/CORB

Le Grande Diable Mammon d'Argent, 1790

human hand with wicks at the fingertips. If a candle burns fast and clean, the money you desire is as good as in the bank—and if the wax drips on the offering, the sum could exceed your expectation. Too rapid a burn, however, indicates the spell won't stick. A sooty, slow burn allows hope but the wealth may be hard to come by and a long time in accumulating. A wick that flares too brilliantly or a candle that tips over is a bad sign: someone is casting a spell against you.

Persian Power

*B*aga is the classical Persian god of prosperity, jewels and other treasures. His name in Sanskrit means "giver," and a lunar month in early Spring was given over to his honor. He is also the patron of fruitful marriages. In Vedic tradition he is known as *Bhaga*.

Gods of Fat City East

*D*aikoku is the Japanese god of having. Fat and prosperous, he sits on sacks of rice, with a bag of jewels on his shoulder. He carries a magic mallet to make subscribers' wishes come true. Not only is he the patron deity of farmers, he's the guy to see when business is shaky or you're personally into deficit spending.

Hotei, Shinto god of chance, is also a roly-poly, smiling figure. Rubbing the belly of a *Hotei* statue is said to bring good luck.

New Year's Sweepstakes

Chimney sweeps (as any Mary Poppins fan can tell you) are lucky. In Eastern Europe, chimney-sweep postcards are sent to mark New Year's Day, a carryover from the folk belief that meeting a chimney sweep on New Year's Day would bring luck throughout the year. The cards sometimes show the sweeps handing over bags of cash to people.

If you believe that soot can be spun into gold, you may also subscribe to the notion that it's auspicious to step into manure on the street.

Luck Rides In

Mexican gamblers rely on *El Secreto de la Virtuosa Herradura*, which is an international grabbag of traditions.

A gold paper cross accompanies a print of St. Martin of Tours, the patron Saint of horse-

men and beggars, known locally as *San Martin Cabellero*. The back story is that this 4th-Century saint was a mounted soldier who once encountered a freezing beggar. Martin slashed his cloak in two and gave half to the mendicant. In a later dream, the beggar was revealed to him as Jesus.

The package also contains a used horseshoe, wrapped in thread and decorated with sequins. The origin of horseshoe luck appears to lie in its magnetic potential to draw coin. It should show wear because folklore promises luck to one who *finds* a horseshoe.

The sack, which is about six inches square, may also contain a Buddha figurine or a Star of David.

Saint Martin and the Beggar, 1599, by El Greco

Tooth Fairies Etc.

In the folklore of many places, whole races of magical creatures live just outside the range of human understanding, and many of these either guard or confer wealth.

Leprechauns and fairies are familiar European tiny ones who have ambivalent dealings with humans, as thieves, guardians and givers of wealth. Fairies, whose power is called "glamour," traditionally bestowed gifts on children—the tooth fairy is their descendant. Leprechauns had pots of gold that a human might be able to claim.

CHAPTER FIVE

SPECULATION

SPECTACLES

Looking back on the great stock market crash of 1929, economist John Kenneth Galbraith noted that the collapse was "implicit in the speculation that went before. The only question concerning that speculation was how long would it last."

When confidence in ever-greater stock prices faltered, Galbraith wrote, the sole reality became falling prices and "a rush, pell-mell, to unload. This was the way past speculative orgies ended. It was the way the end came in 1929. It is the way speculation will end in the future."

History is littered with the empty wallets of those who thought that they had caught the UP elevator and that the sky had become the limit for their investments. Humanity has a weakness for speculation, an eternal hope for the easy buck, and the inevitable result is, as Galbraith observed, falling prices and ruin for many. The sad lessons in all these historic crashes is this: Almost no one ever sees it coming.

CRASHING THROUGH THE TULIPS

In 1556, the scholar-statesman-naturalist Augier Ghislain de Busbecq shipped some seeds and flower bulbs from Turkey to Europe, thereby setting the stage for one of the stranger speculative fevers of all time: Tulipmania.

Before that century was out, tulips were the delight of those fortunate Europeans who could afford rare and expensive garden plants. One London apothecary spent 20 years trying to collect every sort of tulip, but a friend concluded the task was like "trying to roll Sisyphus' stone, or number the sands."

For a time, tulip cultivation remained a hobby of the rich; in 1624 a bulb of the *Semper Augustus* variety sold for 1,200 florins in Holland—a sum that would have purchased 120 sheep or a set of 20 silver drinking cups. But by 1633, ordinary Dutch citizens had begun to buy cheaper bulbs to reproduce and sell.

Then speculation ignited: The Dutch, who had developed an active stock trade, and had long since begun to trade options, went mad over tulip bulbs. By mid-1635, tulip futures were being traded, based on how many new bulbs a single bulb would produce. In a matter of months, a single *Semper Augustus* bulb fetched almost 5,000 florins, with a coach and pair of horses tossed into the bargain.

Speculation was never in fuller bloom. As Buckner Hollingsworth observed in *Flower Chronicles,* "a nobleman might buy 2,000 florins' worth of bulbs from a chimney sweep who did not have any, and would then sell them to a farmer who did not want any, but who planned to sell them in turn to somebody else." Traders could make 60,000 florins' profit a month.

Immoderate love of flowers had made history before: Romans had been enchanted by roses, to the point that the poet Horace complained that good farmland was being turned over to rosebushes. But nothing matched tulipmania.

It all came crashing down in 1637 when a shipment of bulbs found no buyers. By that time, homes and businesses had been sold or mortgaged to raise funds for tulip speculation, and many citizens were ruined.

Francisco Pizarro; Navigator and Conquistador by Amable-Paul Coutan (1792-1837)

In Search of El Dorado

The Americas might have remained a bosky curiosity were it not for one fact: There was gold here—enough to make Spain a world power and make beasts of some of the early explorers.

When Columbus returned from his first voyage, he reported, "The gate to the gold and pearls is now open." Not that he had actually seen any of either, but he knew what his backers wanted to hear.

The legends explorers heard from the natives were surely alluring: The Muisca Indians told of *El Dorado,* a man who dressed in gold from head to toe for a religious ceremony and who lived in the city—mythical, as it turned out—of Manoa, supposedly near Bogota where even the cooking pots were of solid gold. The Europeans heard, too of the Seven Cities of Cibola, supposedly situated in what is now the southwestern United States. These fabulously wealthy towns were also known in legend as the Seven Cities of Gold.

Some gold-hungry explorers were doomed to disappointment: Francisco Vasquez de Coronado roamed the Southwest looking for golden cities, but had to be content with finding the Colorado and Rio Grande rivers and the Grand Canyon, and with crossing the Continental Divide and much of the Great Plains.

Hernando De Soto had a similar experience in the American southeast: Someone had told him that Florida was "the land of gold," and he spent four fruitless years searching there, extending his quest to what is now Georgia, both Carolinas, Alabama, Tennessee, Arkansas, Mississippi and Louisiana. He was the European discoverer of the Mississippi River, and it became the final stop on his journey when he died of a fever.

But others did find gold, in quantities almost as great as the wildest tales. Hernando Cortes conquered Mexico, looted it of tons of gold, and destroyed Aztec civilization.

When conquistador Francisco Pizarro captured the Inca ruler Atahualpa, the prisoner offered to cover the floor of a 17-by-22-foot room with gold. This didn't impress his captors, so Atahualpa increased the offer: He'd

God of death.

fill the room with gold as high as he could reach. His jailers accepted this offer, and a room was duly filled with gold and silver treasures. The Spainards melted the precious metals into about 124 tons of ingots for easy shipment home. Later, they strangled Atahualpa.

The conquistadors did not always have an easy time of it; while Cortes was looting Mexico City, the fierce Shuars of Ecuador defeated a Spanish expedition. Although the Shuar were adept at shrinking human heads, they decided on a more fitting fate for their captives. They had noticed that the Spaniards were avid for gold. "You are very greedy," they told them, as they poured molten gold down their throats.

BUBBLE BATH

The South Sea Bubble was founded on debt. In 1711, the South Sea Trading Company purchased £9,000,000 of the British government's obligations, on which the government guaranteed six percent interest. As part of the deal, the English merchant firm also obtained exclusive trading rights in South America, from which it hoped to reap huge profits.

One underrated detail was that London was not in political control of this particular continent. The

An Emblematical Print on the South Sea Bubble by William Hogarth

Spanish did agree, however, to let England monopolize the importation of African slaves to their colonies—a trade area as financially risky as it is morally abhorrent.

While waiting for the government to start paying interest and for South American gold to magically flow in, the company offered £300 shares, and these skyrocketed in price, reaching £1,000 within months.

Sir Isaac Newton doubled his initial £7,000 stake in six weeks, then sold out. But he impulsively bought in again and lost £20,000. "I can calculate the motions of heavenly bodies but not the madness of people," he acknowledged.

The early success of South Sea shares touched off a lunatic wave of speculation throughout the British Isles. Everyone was offering shares in every harebrained venture imaginable. Charles Mackay, in his classic *Extraordinary Popular Delusions and the Madness of Crowds*, listed four pages of crazy stock offerings. Here's a sampling of schemes promising fast fortunes:

Reviving and carrying on a whale fishery in Greenland
Trading in hair
Paving the streets of London
Drying malt by hot air
Extracting silver from lead
Buying and fitting out ships to suppress pirates

> "Life is so unlike theory."
> —ANTHONY TROLLOPE

Two IPOs of the South Sea bubble era truly surpass understanding. The offering of one company was called "Globe Permits," which were pieces of playing cards stamped with the wax seal of the Globe Tavern and marked "Sail Cloth Permits." At 60 guineas each—far more than the average family earned a year—they gave the bearer the right to someday invest in a sailcloth concern. An even more mysterious offering—but one that may be recognizable to contemporary dot.com flyers—announced that it was "for carrying on an undertaking of great advantage; but nobody to know what it is."

Meanwhile, the South Sea Trading Company bought more government debt in 1719, and collapsed in 1720. A pamphlet published in Boston the next year summed up the consequences: "Many poor Families have been ruined, brought to Poverty, and turned beggars. The Trade of the City of London, one of the finest in the World, hath been very much shortened, few Ships have been built, or fitted to Sea During the Reign of the South-Sea Company."

Gold in Them Thar Hills

"The accounts of the abundance of gold in that territory [California] are of such extraordinary character as would scarcely command belief were they not corroborated by authentic reports of officers in the public service."— President James Polk, December 1848

When gold was discovered in California, the rush was so mad that there were traffic jams on the Oregon-California Trail; lines of wagons stretched from horizon to horizon for days at a time; people near the back had to fashion goggles to keep dust out of their eyes. Prairie along the way was overgrazed, and there were so many camp latrines along the route that water supplies were polluted.

At the beginning of the journey, water was plentiful and supplies were cheap—a barrel of flour was $4. Out past the last general stores, flour cost a dollar for a pint—if you could find it.

A few sharp Californians sent water wagons east to greet the eager prospectors. When water ran short, men paid as much as $100 for a glass of it.

Back in Indiana, another sharper sold salve: You rubbed it on your body, rolled down a hill, and gold (or silver, for which there was a separate salve) would stick to you. All you had to do was scrape it off and retire wealthy.

Black Magic

Oil wasn't called "black gold" for nothing; it provoked rushes as frantic as the searches for precious metal.

After the Civil War, thousands rushed to the Pennsylvania oil fields, where one early well returned $15,000 for each dollar invested. In January 1865, drillers hit oil in the tiny farm community of Pithole; within six months four wells were producing 2,000 barrels a day.

A farm that brought $1.3 million in July went for $2 million in September. By that time, the population of Pithole had hit 15,000; there were more than 50 hotels and scores of boardinghouses in town.

But the wells began to run dry just at that moment, and the speculators ran. By January 1866, Pithole was a ghost town. In 1878, the farm that had brought $2 million was auctioned off for $4.37.

Mountain Jack and a Wandering Miner, by E. Hall Martin, c. 1850

Many made money in novel ways during the gold rush. One woman socked away $18,000 by cooking meals in her sole pot. Women were so scarce that one man who got married charged less fortunate brethren $5 to look at his bride.

The service industry boomed: There was a need for secure banks and secure transportation, and Henry Wells and William Fargo got rich providing it.

An 1871 list of San Francisco's wealthiest men, and the source of their money, is instructive:

Leland Stanford, Central Pacific Railroad	$10,000,000
Ben Holladay, stagecoaches	$ 7,500,000
Michael Reese, real estate and loans	$ 4,000,000
John Parrott, real estate	$ 4,000,000
Darius Ogden Mills, Bank of California	$ 3,500,000
James Lick, pianos and real estate	$ 3,000,000
Alvinza Hayward, Mother Lode goldmine	$ 3,000,000
James Phelan, liquor and real estate	$ 2,500,000
Lloyd Tevis, Wells Fargo & Co.	$ 2,000,000
James Ben Ali Haggin, Wells Fargo & Co.	$ 2,000,000
William C. Ralston, Bank of California	$ 1,500,000

> "Fortune lies upon the surface of the earth as plentiful as the mud in our streets. We look for an addition within the next four years equal to at least One Thousand Million of Dollars to the gold in circulation."
> —HORACE GREELEY, *New York Tribune*

The search for gold could be gut-wrenching hard work with pick and shovel, but it was often as easy as sloshing sand around in a pan, or picking up nuggets. And gold did make some miner-millionaires, some from nothing at all. John Mackay arrived in Virginia City, Nev., dead broke. Ten years later, he hosted a dinner at which 10,000 magnums of champagne were drained. When he died at the dawn of the 20th Century, one of the richest men in the West, his assistants were unable to estimate his fortune within $20 million.

THE TRAIL OF NINETY-EIGHT

Gold! We leaped from our benches. Gold! We sprang from our stools.
Gold! We wheeled in the furrow, fired with the faith of fools.
Fearless, unfound, unfitted, far from the night and the cold,
Heard we the clarion summons, followed the master-lure—Gold!

. . . Farewell! We cried to our sweethearts; little we cared for their tears.
Farewell! We cried to the humdrum and the yoke of the hireling years;
Just like a pack of schoolboys, and the big crowd cheered us goodbye.
Never were hearts so uplifted, never were hopes so high . . .

And one man wanted a castle, another a racing stud;
A third would cruise in a palace yacht like a red-necked prince of blood.
And so we dreamed and we vaunted, millionaires to a man,
Leaping to wealth in our visions ere the long trail began . . .

The greed of the gold possessed us; pity and love were forgot;
Covetous visions obsessed us; brother with brother fought.
Partner with partner wrangled, each one claiming his due;
Wrangled and halved their outfits, sawing their boats in two . . .
—ROBERT SERVICE

RUNNING HALF-BAKED TO ALASKA

On August 17, 1896, three Yukon characters—Skookum Jim, Tagish Charlie and George Carmack—discovered gold on Rabbit Creek, sparking the Klondike gold rush. When a newspaper report noted that a steamer had left the Yukon for Seattle laden with "more than a ton of solid gold aboard," 100,000 *cheekchakos* (greenhorns) swarmed to Skagway to begin the horrifying trek up the infamous Chilkoot Trail to the Klondike goldfields.

Some got rich, but again they weren't often miners. Belinda Mulroney threw her last 50 cents into the Yukon River when she arrived in the Klondike, vowing to never need such small change again. She sold rubber boots, cotton goods and hot water bottles at a 600 percent mark-up, built a roadhouse, owned six mining properties by the end of a year, and built the Fairview Hotel.

Stock Shock

Long-Term Capital Management thought it had found something akin to the Philosopher's Stone or the Perpetual-Motion Machine: Profit Without Risk. And it wasn't only John Meriwether, who founded the high-flying hedge fund on the theories of several honored academics, who believed it: All the major financial houses wanted a piece of this millennium-end sure thing, which was predicated on the belief that small price differences in stock options could be predicted with great certainty and exploited for great profit.

LCTM was heavily leveraged, meaning it was betting with borrowed money—as much as $100 borrowed for every real dollar of equity. If you wanted to play, the minimum investment was $10 million.

When economic temblors struck Asia and Eastern Europe in 1998, the professors' refined logic came apart and LTCM quickly went something like $10 billion in the hole.

The resulting shock wave threatened so many monied people and institutions that the Federal Reserve decided LCTM was too big to fail, and jawboned a group of big financial institutions into ponying up $3.6 billion to keep the sinking ship afloat.

> "You don't want no pie in the sky when you die. You want something here on the ground while you're still around."
> —MUHAMMED ALI

MILLENNIAL MANIA

As the 21st Century dawned, stock-speculation fever raged among the masses. Any internet-linked individual could exercise the inalienable right to pursue happiness on Wall Street—or in almost any market place—without leaving home.

As was to be expected, this left moralists (and some economists) wringing their hands over the explosive growth of the stock market, particularly—as the media never ceased to repeat—"the technology-heavy NASDAQ index."

The optimists, however, spoke of a "new paradigm" that meant the market and economy would never crash again.

They refused to be haunted by the words that Fred Hartley, the head of Unocal, spoke in 1984. Locked then in one of the decade's brutal leveraged-buyout struggles, he said, "This speculative binge, this chain letter, must eventually collapse, leaving wreckage of ruined companies, lost jobs, reduced U.S. oil production, failed banks and savings and loans, and government bailouts, not to mention unemployment and empty buildings."

He was right on most counts.

Will the 21st Century be the first to defy financial gravity? It's time, ladies and gentlemen, to place your bets.

NET. NOTHING

The California-based NetJ.com company, which has no day-to-day operations, disclosed in its Security and Exchange Commission (SEC) filing that its business plan was to seek one or more profitable business combinations or acquisitions to secure profit for shareholders. Its public offering of stock nonetheless was a success. A NetJ share, which once had been valued at 31 cents, rose to $8.87 in March, 2000, several weeks after its initial offering. Price sank to the $2 level as NetJ.com apparently remained in the business of doing nothing.

CHAPTER SIX

TELLING

TALES

"Golden Eggs" engraving by Edmund Evans for
Baby's Own Aesop by Walter Crane, 1887.

Avarice, in Aesop's book, is a trap that may land you in the lap of nothing. Or, as 20th-Century fabulist Truman Capote cautioned: Beware of answered prayers.

The historical jury is out on whether there was an actual Aesop, a Greek who collected folk tales in the 6th Century B.C., and artfully stuffed them into a collection of parables, often starring animals. The stories come from many lands, and the oldest, extant retelling of them is in a 2nd-Century collection of verses by Babrius.

Regardless of whether he existed as more than a byline, Aesop was the Walt Disney of the ancient world. The fables attributed to him have pulsed with life and plausible truths for over two millennia. We're still debating the wisdom of killing the goose that lays golden eggs, as any student of late 20th-Century corporate takeovers can tell you.

Real-life lessons were probably no clearer to ancient Greeks than contemporary ones are to us. The fables are not the antique equivalents of Harvard Business School case histories; they were and remain moral guides based on centuries of observance of human foibles and their probable consequences.

Perils of Overreaching

Often, Aesop's is not the only version of an oft-told story. For instance, one tale features a boy who reached into a jar of hazelnuts and grabbed so many that he couldn't get his hand out. Unwilling to open his fingers, he laments his ill luck. A bystander remarks, "Come, my boy, don't be so greedy. Be content with half the nuts and you'll be able to take your hand out easily."

In India, the fall guy of the story is a monkey who becomes stuck after reaching into a small hollow of a rock for grains of wheat. Unable to withdraw all the wheat, the monkey gives up and goes away hungry. (Apparently, monkeys really are as foolish as humans. Monkey hunters often succeed by digging holes with narrow necks and placing bait inside them. Monkeys who take the bait cannot bring themselves to let go—even when a dangerous homo sapiens approaches.)

Aesop also tells this related fable: A mouse squirms into a container of grain and eats so much that he can't fit through the opening to leave. A weasel advises, "The only way to escape is to wait until you're as lean and hungry as you were when you went in."

Another Aesop tale suggests it's a good idea to cooperate—and give the king of the jungle his due. A fox goes to work for a lion, pointing out prey for the lion to kill and share with him. But the fox comes to resent the lion's share, and quits to hunt alone. The next day, the fox is so absorbed in his solitary struggle to carry off a sheep that a farmer and his dog catch and kill him.

The old Greek philosopher—or whoever his ghostwriters were—also promoted joint venture in a tale with a happy ending. On a hot, parched day, a lion and a goat reach a small fountain. They argue so long about when and how much each might drink, that vultures start hovering. When they notice the grim birds overhead, they decided it is better to cooperate than to be food for scavengers.

A dog is the loser in a scene that shows the folly of greed and punishes theft. It opens with a happy hound crossing a river with a stolen piece of meat in his mouth. The dog, catching sight of his reflection in a pool, thinks he sees a canine rival. Snapping at him in hope of grabbing extra dinner, he irretrievably drops the treasure in his mouth. One moral: Reach for the shadow, lose the substance.

The DOG & the shadow

IS image the Dog did not know,
Or his bone's, in the pond's painted show:
"T'other dog," so he thought,
"Has got more than he ought;
So he snapped, & his dinner saw go!

·GREED·IS·SOMETIMES·
CAUGHT·BY·ITS·
OWN·BAIT

Woodcut print from *Baby's Own Aesop.*

What's Worth Keeping

Deconstructing folklore uncovers layers of meaning. At least one Aesopian tale embodies freedom's cry. One night a starving wolf encountered a farm dog. "How do you manage to stay so sleek and fit?" the wolf asked.

"I guard my master's house, and he feeds me," the dog answered, and invited the wolf to join him. The wolf happily trotted beside his new colleague until he noticed a mark on his friend's neck. Asked about it, the dog said it probably came from the collar he wore when he was chained up during the day.

Horrified, the wolf declaimed, "A dry crust and freedom is better than luxury with a chain around my neck," and fled.

Or consider the implicit day-trader tip in the tale of the fisherman who, after a long day at his empty nets, caught a small fish. "Spare me now, and catch me later when I'm bigger and more fit to eat," inveigled his catch.

The fisherman responded, "Do you take me for a fool?"

Moral: Only a dolt would pass up certain gain for an uncertain profit.

Other Aesopian morality plays reinforce this notion.

A herder drove his goats into a cave during a storm and found a herd of wild goats taking shelter there. He decided that the wild animals were better than his own, and fed them the food he'd brought along. By the time the weather cleared, his goats had starved to death. And the wild ones fled into the hills when the sun appeared.

CRYING OVER SPILLED MILK

A maid, carrying home a pail of milk, calculated that the money it would bring when sold would buy many eggs, which would produce many chickens, which would bring in enough money for her to buy a beautiful gown to wear to the fair, where all the young men would court her. Lost in this dream of future glory, she stumbled and spilled the milk.

This story concludes with the famous point about poultry and the rest of life: Don't count your chickens until they're hatched.

Many variations on the milkmaid's mishap exist.

Scheherezade, in *A Thousand and One Nights*, recites the tale of a barber whose brother inherited some fine glassware that he placed on a table to admire. He hoped to sell his inheritance for a handsome sum that he could catapult into a magnificent fortune. In his feverish dream of riches to come, he kicked over the table, breaking all the glasses.

A medieval Jewish tale featured a golem whose royal master gave him a daily ration of honey. Instead of eating it, he saved it in a jar. While whirling in a fantasy about the wealth the filled jug would bring, he shattered it.

The *Pantschatantra* tells the story this way: Svabhavakripana begged money and bought a bowl of rice gruel, which he hung above his bed. He gazed at it, thinking that if famine came he could sell it for a hundred pieces of silver. With that, he could buy two goats, which he could breed into a herd and trade for cattle whose calves he could trade for buffalo, and those for horses. His reverie led him to imagine a rich wife and a kick aimed at his wife when she failed to pay attention. The kick, of course, strikes the bowl of gruel.

From the Brothers Grimm comes the folktale of Lean Lisa, who was fixated on finding a florin to start her fortune until her husband almost smothered her with a pillow to stop her nattering about wealth.

There are similar legends from Sweden to the Ozarks.

Manda Lamétrie, fermière, 1887, by Alfred Roll

SIGN LANGUAGE

Decoding folktale morality became a high art in Renaissance "emblem books" that squeezed interpretation into a motto or headline, accompanied by a picture and short explanation. The books were used as texts in church academies. Some emblem images decorated popular pageants.

Andrea Alciato, an Italian moral philosopher, first published his influential and much-copied *Book of Emblems* in 1531 in Latin. In 1586, Geffrey Whitney published his English verse, *A Choice of Emblemes*, liberally borrowing Alciato's engravings. The 16th-Century consensus is that a miser is a donkey.

IN AVAROS

Septitius ritche, a miser moste of all
Whose livings large and treasure did exceede:
Yet to his goodes he was so much in thrall
That still he used on beetes and rapes to feede.
So of his stoare, the sweete he never knewe,
And longe did robbe his bellie of his due . . .
—GEFFRY WHITNEY Emblem 18,
A Choice of Emblemes, 1586

MISERABLE MISER

"Septitius [is] the richest of them all, no man has vaster lands than he. He has denied both his own enjoyment and prepared his table; he devours nothing but beets and tough turnips. With what shall I compare this man whom wealth makes poor? Why not an ass? Yes, that's it. For [although] an ass bears on its back costly victuals, he's a pauper who feeds himself on brambles and tough weeds."

—ANDREA ALCIATO, Emblem 86, *Book of Emblems*, 1531, translated by Wm. Barker, Mark Feltham and Jean Guthrie, Memorial University, Newfoundland

Book of Emblems
woodprint, 1531

Last Words

There may be cold comfort in the Aesopian fable of the man who converted his possessions into a lump of gold and buried it in the ground. He visited his hiding site regularly until the day he found that the nugget had been stolen. A friend, hearing him bewail his loss, suggests the miser replace the lost nugget with a stone: "Since you never meant to spend your wealth, the stone will be just as good as the gold."

A Russian folktale tells of a man who was niggardly in the extreme: Realizing that his death was near, he heaped all of his gold on a table, sat down, and began to eat it. He did not stop until he had swallowed every piece. Then he died smiling.

His sons had him decently laid out, and the priest came to sit with the body. At the stroke of midnight, Satan appeared. He seized the corpse and shook it violently. Gold spilled from the gaping mouth, clinking and glinting in the firelight. When the last coin had fallen to the floor, the devil carried the body to the doorway, turned to the priest and smiled.

"The gold is yours," he said. "But the sack is mine."

Woodcut print from *Baby's Own Aesop*.

Big Picture

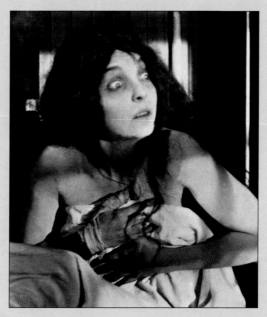

Greed

ZaSu Pitts (Mrs. McTeague) is too bedeviled by avarice to sleep. From *Greed* (MGM).

You might think that sex gets the lead role in filmdom, but wait: Not only does greed drive crime film, it also grins in adventure tales and winks through many romances. Think of

Topkapi and *To Catch a Thief* without the jewel thieves, *The Sting* without loot baiting its hooks, *Ninotchka* without the capitalist creature comforts of Paris, and the James Bond sagas without the trappings of luxury.

Film connoisseurs believe that one of the great films of all time was *Greed* itself, the 1924 silent by Erich von Stroheim.

The script was an adaptation of the Frank Norris novel, *McTeague*, a tale about a couple ruined after the wife wins $5,000 in a lottery and becomes obsessed with money. Norris based the novel on the actual 1893 murder, in San Francisco, of Sarah Collins by her drunkard husband, who wanted her to give him money.

By the film's end, McTeague has murdered his wife, taken the money and fled to Death Valley. His former friend, Marcus, joins a posse in pursuit, hoping to collect a $100 reward. McTeague finally kills Marcus, but in doing so becomes handcuffed to the corpse: He has the $5,000 in gold, but no water and no way to escape death in the desert.

Greed hit a raw nerve in America when it was first released. One review called it "the filthiest, vilest, most putrid picture ever in the history of the motion picture business. In Austria, where Erich von Stroheim comes from, they may enjoy this picture, but I doubt if a single normal American can be found to feel that way about it."

Von Stroheim's original ran four hours (cut down from eight), but studio heads had it chopped to two. The missing hours have become a Holy Grail to greedy film buffs.

CHINATOWN

PARAMOUNT, 1974

"That dam's a con job . . . They're conning LA into building it, but the water's not gonna go to LA. It's coming right here . . . everything you can see, everything around us. They're blowin' these farmers out of their land and picking it up for peanuts. You have any idea what this land would be worth with a steady water supply? About thirty million more than they paid for it."
—JAKE GITTES (Jack Nicholson)

There are few films as dark as this tale of profiteering on Los Angeles' growth (a story not far from the truth) and of the incestuous lust and murderous will of millionaire Noah Cross (John Huston), who's behind the land swindle. "Course I'm respectable," Cross tells Gittes, while trying to get him to double-cross his client. "I'm old. Politicians, ugly buildings and whores all get respectable if they last long enough. I'll double your fee and pay you ten thousand dollars."

The scene concludes with this back-and-forth.

Gittes: "How much are you worth?"
Cross: "I've no idea. How much do you want?"
Gittes: "I just want to know what you're worth. Over ten million?"
Cross: "Oh my, yes."

Gittes: "Why are you doing it? How much better can you eat? What can you buy that you can't already afford?"

Cross: "The future, Mr. Gittes. The future."

The Treasure of the Sierra Madre

WARNER BROTHERS, 1946

" **G**old's a devilish sort of thing. You start out to tell yourself you'll be satisfied with 25,000 handsome smackers worth of it, so help me Lord and cross my heart. Fine resolution. After

Humphrey Bogart plays Dobbs who insists, "Gold don't carry any curse."

months of sweating yourself silly and growing short on provisions and finding nothing, you finally come down to 15,000, and then ten. Finally, you say, "Lord, let me just find $5000 worth and I'll never ask for anything more the rest of my life.

"I tell you, if you were to make a real strike, you couldn't be dragged away. Not even the threat of a miserable death would keep you from trying to add 10,000 more. Ten, you want 25. Twenty-five, you want to get fifty. Fifty, a hundred."
—HOWARD (Walter Huston)

These and other words of wisdom fall on the deaf ears of Fred Dobbs (Humphrey Bogart), a skunk who has one foot in the gutter of Tampico, Mexico. Dobbs insists, "Gold don't carry any curse. It all depends on whether or not the guy who finds it is the right guy. The way I see it, gold can be as much of a blessing as a curse."

The Sierra Madre treasure proves him dead wrong.

"He who hesitates is poor."
—MEL BROOKS in *The Producer*, 1968

THE THIRD MAN

BRITISH LION/LONDON FILMS, 1949

"Nobody thinks in terms of human beings. Governments don't; why should we? They talk about the people and the proletariat; I talk about the suckers and the mugs. It's the same thing. They have their five-year plans; so have I."
  —HARRY LIME (Orson Welles)

Thus does the war profiteer Lime excuse his racket (he's stealing penicillin from Vienna children's hospitals to sell on the black market) to Holly Martins (Joseph Cotten), his sap of an American friend. The two have met on an enormous Ferris wheel, where Lime can talk without being heard.

At the top of the wheel, looking down on the people far below, he tempts Martins as Jesus tempted Satan in the desert: "Victims? Don't be melodramatic. Look down there. Would you feel any pity if one of those *dots* stopped moving forever? If I offered you £20,000 for every dot that stopped, would you really, old man, tell me to keep my money? Or would you calculate how many dots you could afford to spare—free of income tax, old man, free of income tax. The only way you can save money these days."

Lime expands his rationalization: "In Italy for thirty years under the Borgias they had warfare, terror, murder and bloodshed, but they produced Michelangelo, Leonardo da Vinci and the Renaissance. In Switzerland they had brotherly love, they had five hundred years of democracy and peace. And what did that produce? The cuckoo clock."

Orson Welles (Lime) rationalizes murderous greed to Joseph Cotten (Martins).

Double Indemnity

PARAMOUNT, 1944

"You're like the guy behind the roulette wheel, watching the customers to make sure they don't crook the house. And then, one night, you get to thinking how you could crook the house yourself, and do it smart... I fought it, only I guess I didn't fight it hard enough. The stakes were $50,000, but they were the life of a man, too, a man who'd never done me any dirt—except

he was married to a woman he didn't care anything about, and I did."
—WALTER NEFF (Fred MacMurray)

The film is full of hardboiled, greed-laced dialogue: Neff asks Phyllis (Barbara Stanwyck), "What did you think I was, anyway? A guy that walks into a good-looking dame's front parlor and says, 'Good afternoon, I sell accident insurance on husbands. Have you got one that's been around a little too long? One you'd like to turn into a little hard cash?'"

Walter's confession recorded, as he bleeds to death, sums up the wages of his sin: "Yes, I killed him. I killed him for money and for a woman. I didn't get the money and I didn't get the woman. Pretty, isn't it?"

WALL STREET

PRESSMAN/AMERICAN ENTERTAINMENT, 1987

"In the days of the free market, when our country was a top industrial power, there was accountability to the stockholder. The Carnegies, the Mellons, the men who built this great industrial empire made sure of it because *it was their money at stake.*

"Today, management has no stake in the company . . . *You* own the company. That's right, you the [Teldar] stockholders. And you are being royally screwed over by these, these *bureaucrats*, with their steak lunches, with their hunting and fishing trips, their corporate jets and golden parachutes . . .

"The new law of evolution in corporate America seems to be survival of the unfittest. Well in my book, you either do it right or you get eliminated. In the last seven deals that I've been involved with, there were 2.5 million stockholders who have made a pretax profit of $12 billion. I am not a destroyer of companies. I am a *liberator* of them. The point is, ladies and gentlemen, that greed, for lack of a better word, is good.

"Greed is right. Greed works. Greed clarifies, cuts through and captures the essence of the evolutionary spirit. Greed in all of its forms—greed for life, for money, for love, for knowl-

edge—has marked the upward surge of mankind.

"Greed—you mark my words—will not only save Teldar Paper, but that other malfunctioning corporation called the U.S.A."

—Corporate raider GORDON GEKKO (Michael Douglas)

CHAPTER EIGHT

Con

Classics

No one, not the most honest and upright among us, hates the idea of getting rich quick. Is this greed? Perhaps.

What is bedrock certain is that this hope for a fast buck is the foundation upon which the swindler builds his airy dream castles, in which he invites each and all to invest.

As history has shown, time and again, there is never any shortage of such investors.

FRENCH FOLLIES

John Law

The author of one of history's great investing fiascos was John Law, a Scotsman who fled England in 1694 after killing a man in a duel. After a few years in the Continent's casinos, he set up a bank in France that made novel uses of paper money and credit. He also set up the Mississippi Company, which promised to exploit the natural wealth of France's American holdings.

Law employed tricks that would be familiar to later generations of schemers. He hired beggars to dress as miners and parade through Paris with mining tools, as if on the way to scoop up the wealth of America. French investors bought the ploy and flocked to Law's bank to plunk down their savings for investment in the New World.

Their investments never went beyond Law's pocket. But his Mississippi stock was so popular, legitimate French ventures starved for want of investment. As Mississippi soared to 20 times its original value, Law, in effect, came to control France's economy and trade. He lived well, on one or another of his 15 estates, until the Mississippi bubble burst in 1720, reducing him and much of France to poverty. He left the country and spent his declining years back where he had begun, at the gaming tables.

A Little Ink Goes A Long Way

Among Queen Victoria's guests in her Golden Jubilee Year of 1887 was the man who stole Arizona. This American adventurer, who liked to introduce himself as James Addison Peralta-Reavis, Baron of Arizonac, was accompanied by his wife, Dona Carmelita Sofia Micaela de Peralta, the heir (it was said) to one of the greatest estates in the New World.

Reavis had a trunkful of documents proving that he and his beloved were the owners of much of the then-territory of Arizona and a hefty chunk of neighboring New Mexico. The property was part of a Spanish royal grant made to the distant ancestors of Dona Carmelita.

Or so the papers said.

The "baron" was an ex-Confederate soldier who had drifted into the real estate business in St. Louis. In 1871, a frontier doctor named George Willing stepped into Reavis' office with a tale of having bought deeds for old Spanish land grants in Arizona from an aged Mexican named Miguel Peralta.

When he took a good look at Dr. Willing's documents, Reavis decided better were needed. Using authentic Mexican documents as models, Reavis confected a long pedigree for his claim, creating an entire family of grandees.

In 1882, Reavis appeared in Tucson claiming to own 18,750 square miles of land, a claim that comprised Phoenix, Mesa, Tempe and such gems as the Silver King mine, which was producing several million dollars' worth of silver a year. The following year, he notified landowners in this realm that they should settle with him or pay the consequences.

Some did settle; the Silver King mine paid $25,000 to clear its title.

After state officials punched holes in his claim, Reavis created Dona Carmelita (her real identity is lost to history) and invented a blood claim to the land for her. Now that Reavis was married to such a rich, classy woman, he promised development of his holdings, and floated a fat IPO to finance it.

Reavis flourished for years but was eventually unmasked. He spent a few years in various prisons, emerging broke in 1898 to wander the streets of Phoenix, a city he once had claimed as his own.

The Man Who Sold the Eiffel Tower Twice!

When it came to playing on greed, Victor Lustig was a virtuoso. The Czech-born con man even took Al Capone: He told the mobster he had a sure-fire scheme that would double his money within sixty days. Capone gave him $50,000 and a warning about what would happen if Lustig didn't deliver.

Two months later, Lustig came back and told Capone the scheme had fallen apart. He then stunned Capone by handing back the $50,000. The killer rewarded Lustig's honesty with a $1,000 "reward" just as the con man had planned.

In 1925, Lustig learned that the French government was giving the Eiffel Tower a hard look, deciding whether to repair it or—*quelle horreur*—tear it down.

Lustig saw an opening. On fake letterhead, he summoned Paris' five leading scrap metal dealers to a meeting at the elegant Hotel Crillon.

There he told them that the Eiffel Tower was to be torn down. No one must know—public outcry would be too great. They were to submit bids in secret; the high bidder would "win" the tower and be allowed to salvage its 7,000 tons of steel.

Lustig chose his victim not by bid size but by gullibility. He contacted the "winner," gave him a "contract," and cashed his check, worth something like $100,000. He then went to ground in Vienna, and watched the Paris

La Fée Électricité, 1953, by Raoul Dufy

newspapers. Incredibly, there was no story about the outrageous swindle: The victim had clearly been too embarrassed to go to the police.

So Lustig went back and ran the con again on *another* of the bidders. This one paid, but squawked when he found out the truth. Lustig fled to America. He went to Alcatraz in 1935 for counterfeiting, and died there in 1947.

Yes Virginia, There Was A Ponzi

It was so simple: In 1920, you could buy a postal coupon for a penny in Spain and cash it in for six cents' worth of stamps in the United States.

The spread was similar between other countries, the result of economic upheaval and a 1906 postal treaty signed by more than sixty nations. The coupons were supposed to be of equal value everywhere; currency fluctuations had made that a fiction.

Upon that spread, Charles Ponzi, an Italian immigrant to the United States, built the scheme that has made his name immortal, a synonym for pyramid-type swindles. Setting up business as The Securities Exchange Company in Boston, he offered investors a 50 percent profit in 45 days.

Financial disclosure rules were simpler then, so Ponzi didn't mention that he had been in jail—in Canada for forgery and in the United States for smuggling illegal aliens. Instead, he

CORBIS

Charles Ponzi

beguiled investors by telling them "I landed in this country with $2.50 in cash and $1,000,000 in hopes, and those hopes never left me."

That was good enough for investors hoping for three dollars on every two they put into Ponzi's scheme. Few stopped to calculate that to make the millions he promised, Ponzi would have to trade hundreds of millions of postal coupons, since each yielded at best a few cents' profit, if that, after the overhead costs of buying, processing and selling the coupons were deducted. He'd have needed to spend decades on line at post offices, to make his investors' dreams come true.

Ponzi had needed to borrow $200 from a furniture dealer to set up his office—but he managed to collect $9.5 million from 10,000 investors before his scheme collapsed and the law closed in on him. While out of federal prison during an appeal of his conviction, he started a pyramid land scheme in Florida.

He tried to flee to Italy after the appeal failed, but was captured, jailed and eventually deported. He died in a charity ward in Rio de Janeiro in 1949, leaving an estate of $75.

Chain of Disappointment

"Pyramid schemes are popular because people are greedy and greed can do wonders to a person's thinking," notes Robert Todd Carroll, a scholar of the phenomenon. "For a person desiring to make a large amount of money from a small investment in a short amount of time, wishful thinking often takes over . . . Wishes become facts. Skeptics become idiots for not getting on board. Desires become reality. Asking questions seems rude and unfriendly. Scam artists know how greed works . . ."

The chain letter is the simplest form of pyramid scheme. You get a letter with a list of, say, ten names. You send $10 to the person at the top, take that name off and add yours to the bottom. You send copies of the new letter to ten friends, with instructions to do the same. When your name gets to the top of the list, you supposedly get a lot of money.

How much money? Anyone who actually stopped to calculate the sum would never send off $10. The letter would have to reach more than 11 billion people for your name to reach the top of every list. Since that's more humans than the earth holds, the chances of vast reward are slight.

In fact, there's enough skepticism (and laziness) in the world to doom pyramids; eventually enough people neglect to participate and the thing collapses. The original swindlers make some money; the suckers lose some. And the cycle begins again.

BEYOND PENNY SWINDLES

GEORGE MORROW, *PUNCH*, SEPTEMBER, 1910

If imitation is the sincerest form of flattery, Ponzi must be basking in his grave, because his dubious calling has been emulated by legions of professional descendants, dedicated to pulling in the suckers and separating them from their life savings.

Ivar Kreuger, who had already built an empire on kitchen matches, welcomed new investors. Rumors hinting that "secret" European accounting practices concealed the true enormity of the Match King's fortune may have encouraged investors to think they could similarly hide some of their profits from tax collectors. Gullible Americans forked over $250 million—until 1932, when banks got wise to his book cooking and stopped lending him money, prompting Kreuger to suicide.

In the 1960s, a group of thieves figured they'd do better inventing a bank than robbing one. The Bank of Sark, headquartered in a room over a pub on this small Channel Island, floated $100 million in fake letters of credit, which were sold to swindlers all over the world to bolster their efforts at rooking the overly optimistic.

OUT OF AFRICA

Nigerian con artists have accomplished a sort of payback for the colonial rip-offs of their continent, the worst of which may have been the 1885 deals struck by the African Lake Company with Nyasa chiefs. The British company's agents wrangled exclusive trade rights for huge mineral-rich land tracts in exchange for clothing scraps—the agreement with Chief Mulima, for example, granted him "one piece of cloth and a pair of shoes." Typically, the trade treaties also gave the company the right to tribal labor supplied by the chiefs and road tolls. Eventually, citizens of the trade lands found they owed allegiance and taxes to Mother England.

Small wonder that Africa's most successful private swindlers have specialized in targeting Europeans, Americans and Canadians. Or perhaps these Nigerians have—like bank robber Willie Sutton—simply reached for where the money is. So far, they've succeeded in taking in some $5 billion through "419 Fraud," named after the relevant section of Nigerian law.

Prospects receive an official-looking letter or fax from Nigeria offering a sweet deal on a business deal, the details (and legality) of which vary. The common element is the request for an advance fee to get the deal going—after which, marks are promised, untold wealth will flow their way. If a recruit bites, "problems" arise that require more cash. Needless to say, the payoff never comes. The 419 scam is thought to be the third largest industry in Nigeria.

> "It was beautiful and simple as all truly great swindles are."
> —O. HENRY

Hollywood Dreaming

Some swindlers are the brightest if not the best, and some dupes have professional stature and glitter galore. Robert S. Trippet used his Home-Stake Production Company, an Oklahoma oil-drilling enterprise, to bilk scores of celebrities for 18 years before everything collapsed in 1973.

Trippet set the stage with flair, when he laid out irrigation pipes and painted them to look like oil pipelines. He offered investors a tax shelter and a 300 percent return—and eventually even drilled some holes. In true Ponzi fashion, he paid early investors with money from those who came later. He paid fees and made loans to accountants and lawyers, who sang his praises.

There was some oil,

Like many others, Barbra Streisand was charmed by a super-slick snake-oil salesman named Robert Trippet.

but not near enough. When Home-Stake collapsed, among the sad investors were Alan Alda, Jack Benny, Bob Dylan, Barbra Streisand, Ozzie Nelson, Mia Farrow, top-ranking executives of Pepsico, Bethlehem Steel, Western Union, General Electric, Citicorp, two U.S. Senators and the former governor of Florida. "I had it checked out by my Harvard-educated New York lawyer, the fastest brain in the East," said Phyllis Diller, another loser.

With Friends Like These . . .

"What if you paid . . . $250 a month which produced a minimum of $5,235 income each month for you, while you watched? . . . Well, that's exactly what would happen if you hired Fortuna Alliance as your personal Marketing Expert." —promotional literature for The Fortuna Alliance.

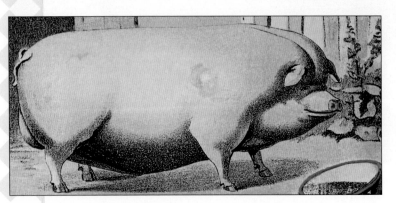

Augie Delgado made the pyramid scheme work in the mid-1990s. The way Delgado explained it, The Fortuna Alliance was going to be a "global buying cooperative," a buying plan for everyday items that would be listed in a catalogue, posted on the Internet.

When you joined, you paid earlier members a percentage. When you brought in new people, they paid you a percentage. Members were also promised special help to protect their gains from taxes, and encouraged to invest more than the $250 minimum.

Although Fortuna had New Age trimmings, Delgado hypnotized investors by waving the Fibonacci Series before them. This was a centuries-old mathematical formula that proved incapable of performing the miracles Augie promised. It did help persuade thousands of people to send in money at a rate that taxed the capabilities of the Fortuna staff in Bellingham, Washington.

The flow was such that no one knows, just yet, how much money Fortuna raked in. When the Federal Trade Commission took action in 1996, labeling Fortuna a pyramid scheme, its agents found $3.6 million, but estimates of the take run as high as $15 million. More than $5 million was traced to Antigua, but the trail went cold there.

Delgado and his associates were forced to return $5.5 million to investors in the United States and 70 other countries.

> "He possesses average intelligence, but is a shallow and parasitic individual who is considerably wrapped up in his own feelings. His ideals of life resolved themselves into money to spend, beautiful women to enjoy, silk underclothes and places to go in style. His social outlook is dominated by recklessness and a craving for action. His only asset as a leader consists of his apparent calmness in times of stress."
> —Pre-sentencing report on Charles (Lucky) Luciano

Not Your Average Boy Scout

In 1985, boy wonder Barry Minkow was honored by the City of Los Angeles for being "a fine entrepreneurial example ... obtaining the status of a millionaire at the age of eighteen."

Four years later he was sentenced to 25 years in jail for crimes connected with his ZZZZ Best rug cleaning company. These included forging $45 million worth of bank checks—which he used to grandly inflate the worth of his business. He showed auditors phony canceled checks for $40 million worth of "restoration jobs" on damaged buildings; the number crunchers had no idea the figures were impossibly high. After a staggeringly high value of his company had been "established," Minkow pushed worthless shares of it off on an unwary public. When he got out of jail (after 7 years), Minkow began lecturing to caution investors about people like him. "Look at the big picture," he warned them. "Get too hung up in the minutiae and you might never see that the entire operation is a fraud."

CHAPTER NINE

GRASPING

AT WORDS

REVENGE, YES; GREED, NO!

Icare for riches to make gifts to friends or to lead a poor man back to health. Else, small aid is wealth to daily gladness; once a man be done with hunger, rich and poor are alike.
—EURIPIDES, *Elektra*

AVARICA

And then came covetousness, I could hardly see him
So hungry and hollow he looked.
He was beetle-browed and thick-lipped also
With two bleared eyes like an old hag.
His cheeks lolled like a leather purse
Much longer than his chin, they trembled with age.
And like a laborer his beard was slobbered with bacon grease.
With a hood on his head, and a lousy hat above,
And in a tawny coat of twelve winters' age
All torn and filthy and full of lice creeping . . .
—WILLIAM LANGLAND, *The Vision of Piers Plowman*

Song of Cash

O bring a gift along,
And black soon greys to white.
Cash makes a contract strong
Cash cannot but be right,
Cash smoothes the roughest wrong,
And stops the fiercest fight,
Cash in the courts holds sway
A law that all obey.
Hey you that judge, I say,
Here comes Lord Cash, make way!

When cash upholds the scales,
Justice is out of date.
Your crooked business fails?
The court will set it straight.
For cash you'll find prevails
To settle the debate.
Bring nothing, and you'll learn
How quickly courts can spurn.
No cash to serve your turn?
At once the judge is stern.
—Anonymous medieval lyricist

SEEKERS & KEEPERS

I speke of avarice and of
Coveitise, of which synne seith saint paul that
The roote of alle harmes is coveitise . . . for soothly, whan the
Herte of a man is confounded in itself and
Troubled, and that the soule hath lost the confort
Of god, thanne seketh he an eydel solas [idle solace]
Of worldly thynges . . .

And the difference bitwixe avarice and coveitise
Is this—coveitise is for to coveite swiche
Thynges as thou hast nat; and avarice is for
To withholde and kepe swiche thynges as thou
Hast, withoute rightful nede. Soothly, this
Avarice is a synne that is ful dampnable;
For al hooly writ curseth it, and speketh agayns
That vice . . . the avaricious
Man hath moore hope in his [chattels] than
In jhesu crist, and dooth moore observance in
Kepynge of his tresor than he dooth to the
Service of jhesu crist.
—GEOFFREY CHAUCER, *The Pardoner's Tale*

Death and the Miser, c. 1485, by Hieronymous Bosch

Sick Joke

He was naturally subject to a kind of disease, which at that time they called lack of money.
—François Rabelais, *Works*, Book II, Ch. 16

The Temple

Money, thou bane of blisse & source of woe,
Whence com'st thou, that thou are so fresh and fine?
I know thy parentage is base and low:
Man found thee poore and dirtie in a mine.

Then forcing thee by fire he made thee bright:
Nay, thou has got the face of man; for we
Have with our stamp and seal transferr'd our right:
Thou art the man, and man but drosse to thee.

Man calleth thee his wealth, who made thee rich
And while he diggs out thee, falls in the ditch.
—George Herbert

RICHES

Since all the riches of the world
May be gifts of the devil and earthly kings,
I should suspect that I worshiped the devil
If I thanked God for worldly things.
—WILLIAM BLAKE

MISER BLUES

Indeed, I am convinced that, had I possessed the whole globe of earth, save one single drachma, which I had been certain never to be master of—I am convinced, I say, that single drachma would have given me more uneasiness than all the rest could afford me pleasure.

To say the truth, between my solicitude in contriving schemes to procure money and my extreme anxiety in preserving it, I have never had one moment of ease while awake nor of quiet when in my sleep . . . And, indeed, I have since learned that the devil will not receive a miser.

—A miser in HENRY FIELDING'S *A Journey From This World to the Next*

PORTRAIT OF A SKINFLINT

Oh! But he was a tight-fisted hand at the grindstone, Scrooge! A squeezing, wrenching, grasping, scraping, clutching, covetous, old sinner! Hard and sharp as flint, from which no steel had ever struck out generous fire; secret, and self contained, and solitary as an oyster.

The cold within him froze his old features, nipped his pointed nose, shriveled his cheek, stiffened his gait; made his eyes red, his thin lips blue; and spoke out shrewdly in his grating voice. A frosty rime was on his head, and on his eyebrows, and his wiry chin. He carried his own low temperature always about with him; he iced his office in the dog days; and didn't thaw it one degree at Christmas.

—CHARLES DICKENS, *A Christmas Carol*

Ebenezer Scrooge encounters miserly Marley's ghost in the 1938 version of *A Christmas Carol.*

Vice Versa

Well, whiles I am a beggar, I will rail,
And say there is no sin but to be rich;
And, being rich, my virtue then shall be
To say there is no vice but beggary.
—WILLIAM SHAKESPEARE, *King John* Act II, Sc. I

Occupational Hazards

But scarce observed, the knowing and the bold
Fall in the general massacre of gold;
Wide-wasting pest! That rages unconfined,
And crowds with crimes the records of mankind;
For gold his sword the hireling ruffian draws,
For gold the hireling judge distorts the laws;
Wealth heaped on wealth, nor truth nor safety buys,
The dangers gather as the treasures rise.
—SAMUEL JOHNSON, *The Vanity of Human Wishes*

Right: *Allegory of Riches* by Simon Vouet (1590-1649)

Two Sides of the Coin

Money is a good servant but a bad master.
—ALEXANDRE DUMAS fils, *La Dame Aux Camélias*

Dipsychus

They may talk as they please about what they call pelf
And how one ought never to think of oneself,
How pleasures of thought surpass eating and drinking.
My pleasure of thought is the pleasure of thinking
How pleasant it is to have money, heigh-ho!
How pleasant it is to have money!
—ARTHUR HUGH CLOUGH

Fashion Statement

Why snatch at wealth, and hoard and stock it?
Your shroud, you know, will have no pocket!
—BETTY PAOLI, *Neueste Gedichte*

Sixth Sense

The value of money is that with it we can tell any man to go to the devil.
It is the sixth sense without which you cannot make use of the other five.
—W. SOMERSET MAUGHAM, *Of Human Bondage*

The Rich Man

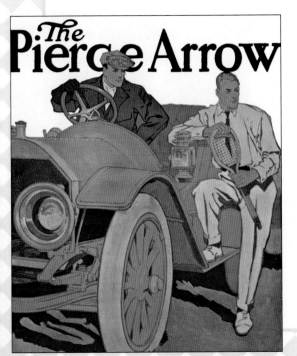

The rich man has his motorcar,
His country and his town estate.
He smokes a fifty-cent cigar
And jeers at Fate.

Yet though my lamp burns low and dim,
Though I must slave for livelihood
Think you that I would change with him?
You bet I would!
—FRANKLIN P. ADAMS

One Perfect Rose

. . . Why is it no one has sent me yet
One perfect limousine, do you suppose?
Ah no, it's always my luck to get
One perfect rose.
—Dorothy Parker

The Rich Are Different

Let me tell you about the rich. They are different from you and me. They possess and enjoy early and it does something to them, makes them soft where we are hard, and cynical where we are trustful, in a way that, unless you are born rich, is difficult to understand. They think deep in their hearts that they are better than we are because we had to discover the compensations of lives for ourselves. Even when they sink below us they still think that they are better than we are. They are different.
—F. Scott Fitzgerald, *The Rich Boy*

SIN SERIES

VOLUME I

Have you read...

SIN SERIES

VOLUME II

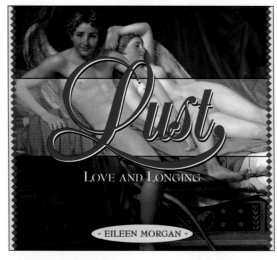

www.redrockpress.com